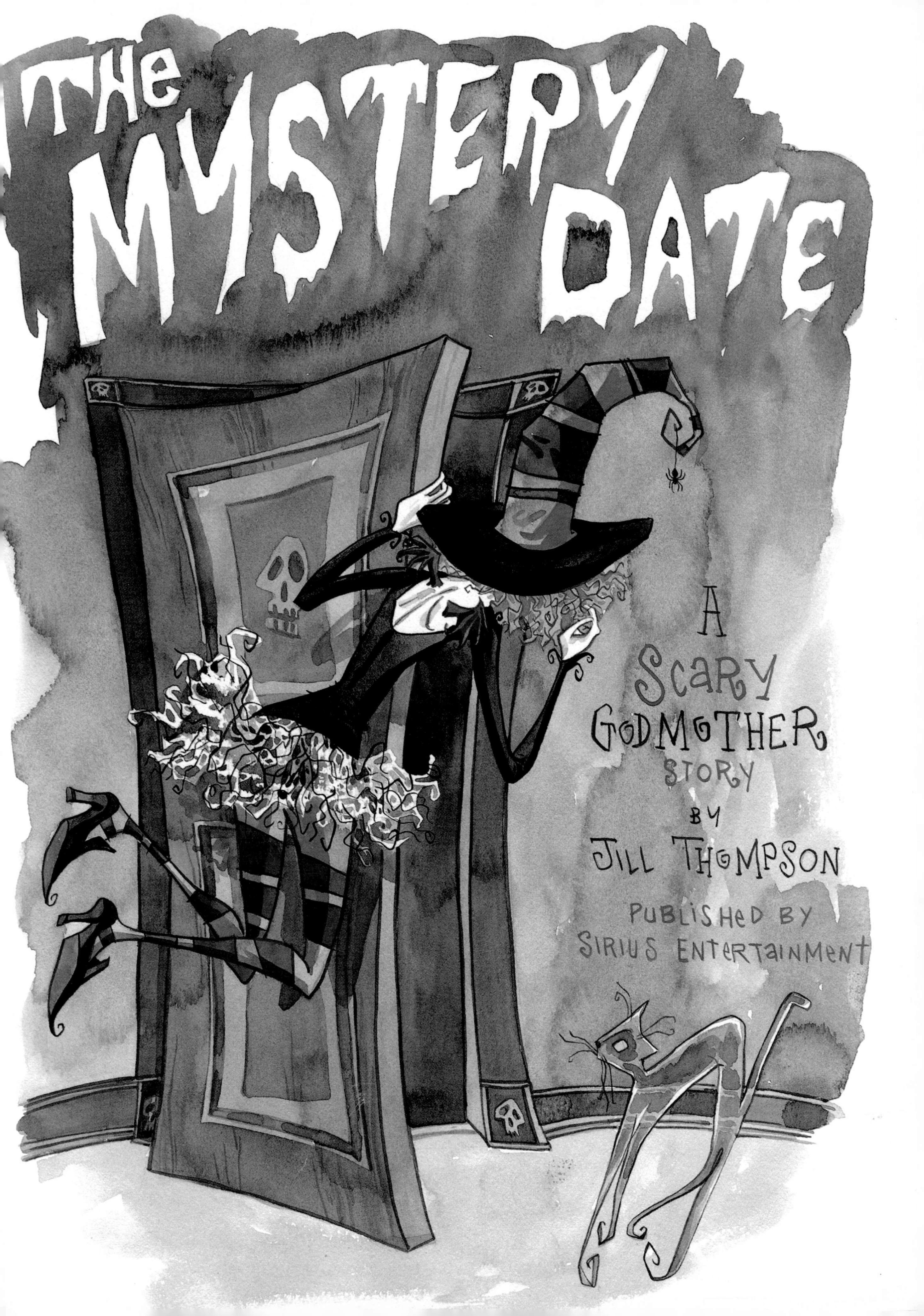
THE MYSTERY DATE
A
SCARY
GODMOTHER
STORY
BY
JILL THOMPSON
PUBLISHED BY
SIRIUS ENTERTAINMENT

SIRIUS

Robb Horan
Publisher

Larry Salamone
President

Joseph Michael Linsner
Art Director

Mark Bellis
Managing Editor

McNabb Studios
Production

Digital Logo Design
Joseph Allen

Book Design
Jill Thompson

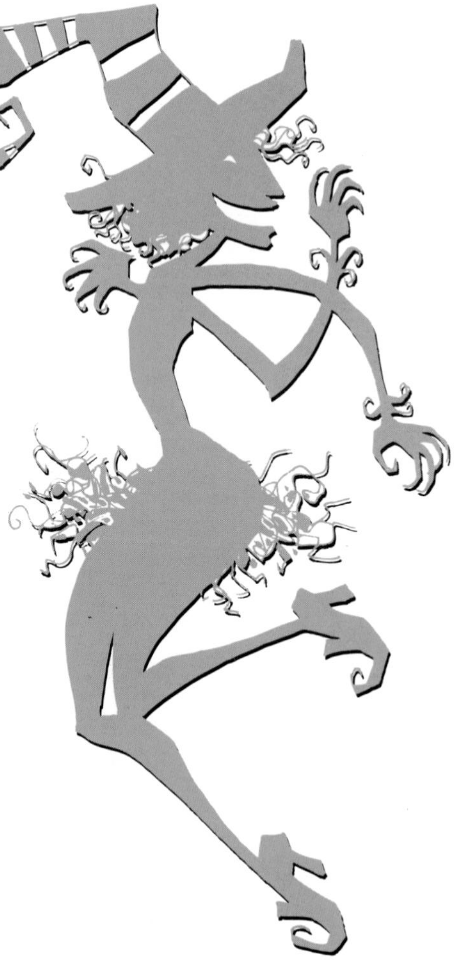

ISBN# 1-57989-026-1
Thompson, Jill
SCARY GODMOTHER / THE MYSTERY DATE / by Jill Thompson
Printed by Brenner Printing
San Antonio, Texas
USA

SCARY GODMOTHER – THE MYSTERY DATE Vol. One. First Printing, September 1999.
Published by Sirius Entertainment, Inc. Correspondence: PO Box 834, Dover, NJ 07802.

DEDiCaTED
to
LuCY

LiAm

and
Abby

Buried Alive! With every turn the car made, Hannah Marie was covered in candy corns, pummeled by pumpkins and battered by bats. As her mom pulled the car into the driveway, Hannah hollered...

If Hannah survived the ride home, she could help her mom with the party plans.

You see, her parents were hosting a Halloween party so big, that the entire neighborhood could come. The block would be closed to traffic so there could be games and dancing in the street! Everyone would decorate their houses and make treats to share. Hannah's mom was in charge of the planning and she checked her guest list to make sure she hadn't forgotten anyone.

Hannah rushed to her room, to make invitations for all of the Monsters she knew.

So, at bedtime, when all of the other kids in town did their best to avoid the Monster under the bed...

...Hannah addressed him by name...

...and the Monster under the bed grumbled back at her.

Visiting the place where Monsters dwell can be a rather tricky procedure, unless of course, you're friends with a Monster or two like little Hannah is. She followed the secret steps as Bug-A-Boo looked on. This is what she did...

The Fright Side is the spooky place where Hannah's Scary Godmother lives. She shares her house with Boozle, her ghostie, Mister Pettibone, the Skeleton in the Closet and Bug-A-Boo, the Monster Under the Bed. They are always doing Halloween things and Hannah can visit them whenever she likes.

Hannah helped move sinister squash outside to the Scary Godmother's porch. Mister Pettibone was quick as a flash, and with only one match, he'd lit up all the jagged-edged faces!

Pulling the pile of party invitations from her pajamas, Hannah asked each of her pals to attend. The creatures roared with dark delight at the prospect of a party.

With Hannah strapped on to her comfy-seat broom, the Scary Godmother flew nearly as high as the moon. Why? To deliver those invitations Fright Side style, of course--by Scare Mail!

The vampires who lived next door to the Scary Godmother accepted...

...as did the Werewolf in the forest (and his mom...).

The patrons of the local watering hole were eager to attend.

During lunch, the kids grew excited as the plans for the party progressed. Hannah's cousin Jimmy listened as they bragged to each other.

There was much to do at the Scary Godmother's house before All Hallow's Eve: scattering spider webbing, squeaking every door, releasing vintage spirits, toasting treats and more. Hannah always lent a helping hand. Amidst the autumn activity, Bug-A-Boo almost went unnoticed, which is hard to do when you're a big, blue Monster!

It was Orson, the Vampire boy, who first noticed the mysterious letter.

The Scary Godmother plucked the paper from Bug-A-Boo's prickly fur and read it.

Mister Pettibone popped out of the closet with an answer.

Bug-A-Boo crunched out a crispy explanation (complete with crumbs)...

...which Mister Pettibone promptly corrected!

Hannah and Orson thought about the Secret Admirer: who could it be? The hatched a plan to identify the monstery, mystery man.

When no one was looking, they sneaked out the door into the Fright Side Night.

The tiny detectives looked far and wide, searching every haunted hang-out on the Fright Side. Just when they thought their luck had run out, they came upon something that caused them to shout...

The Monster Truck Rally was a Frightful Phantom Fest. Monster men brought their mean machines and put them to the test. Surely the Scary Godmother's secret admirer was in this creepy crowd. Dastardly devils, enthusiastic ectoplasm, rambunctious revenants, wild werewolves--you name it and it was there!

Like flies at a picnic, they flitted around, dropping choice tidbits: gossip unbound! A little whisper here, and a bit of stretched-truth there...and they set their plan in motion.

Sure they were fibs, but a few, harmless, little, white lies wouldn't cause any trouble--would they?

As they took to the skies, the conspirators congratulated themselves on a job quite well done...

...unaware of just what their work had begun...

...unaware of how Monsters love competition for fun!

And as quick as a flash, once the word got around...eligible Monsters shambled their way into town!

With moans, groans and grumbles, in groups of two, three and four...they made their way up to the Scary Godmother's door.

They camped out on her doorstep...

...cooked her nine breakfast treats.

18

They lie down in some puddles...

...to keep mud off her feets.

They made monster music...

...to serenade her at night.

They trampled her garden with their wrestling fights!

While watching T.V...

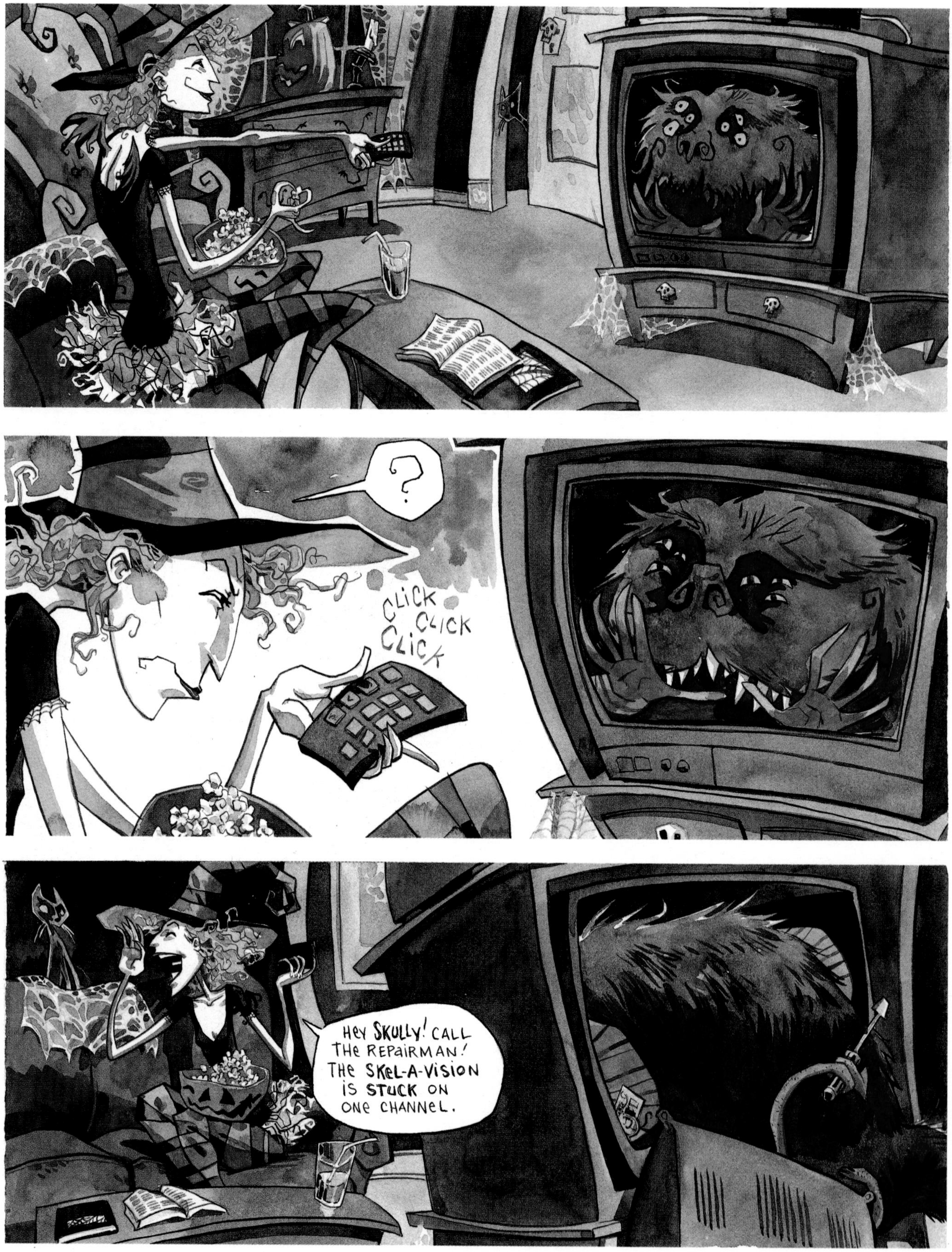
?
CLICK CLICK CLICK
Hey SKULLY! CALL THE REPAIRMAN! THE SKEL-A-VISION IS STUCK ON ONE CHANNEL.

...or taking a bath...

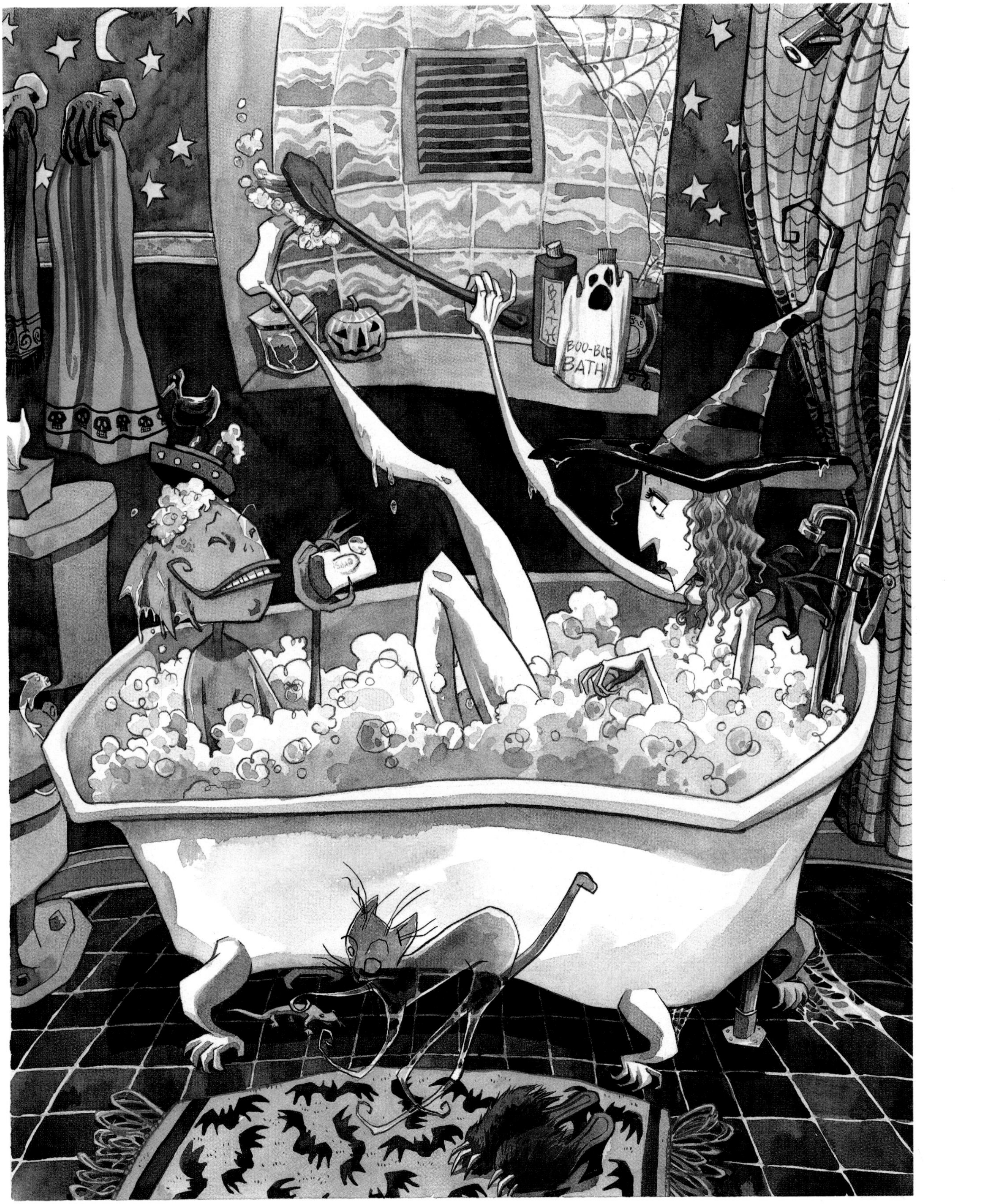
SOAP
BATH
BOO-BLE
BATH

...Monsters popped up in Scary Godmother's path.

And on her way home from the gross-ery store...

...the confused, little spookstress could take it no more!

25

The Scary Godmother frantically huffed and puffed her way back home.

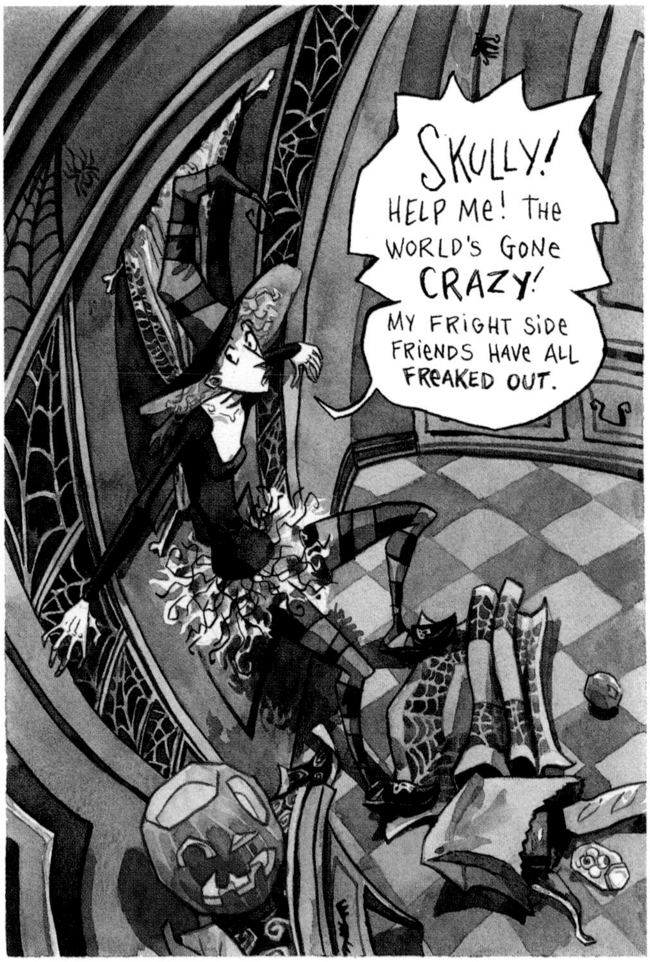
SKULLY! HELP ME! THE WORLD'S GONE CRAZY! MY FRIGHT SIDE FRIENDS HAVE ALL FREAKED OUT.

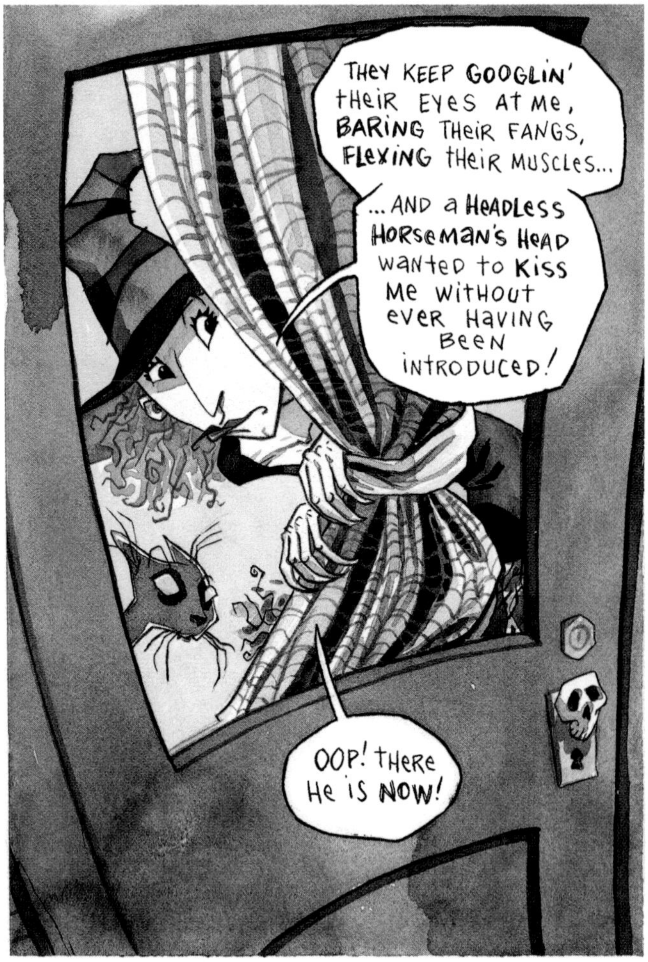
THEY KEEP GOOGLIN' THEIR EYES AT ME, BARING THEIR FANGS, FLEXING THEIR MUSCLES...
...AND A HEADLESS HORSEMAN'S HEAD WANTED TO KISS ME WITHOUT EVER HAVING BEEN INTRODUCED!
OOP! THERE HE IS NOW!

Skully Pettibone, the Skeleton in the Closet, was the keeper of all secrets. He popped out of the armoire to clarify the situation.

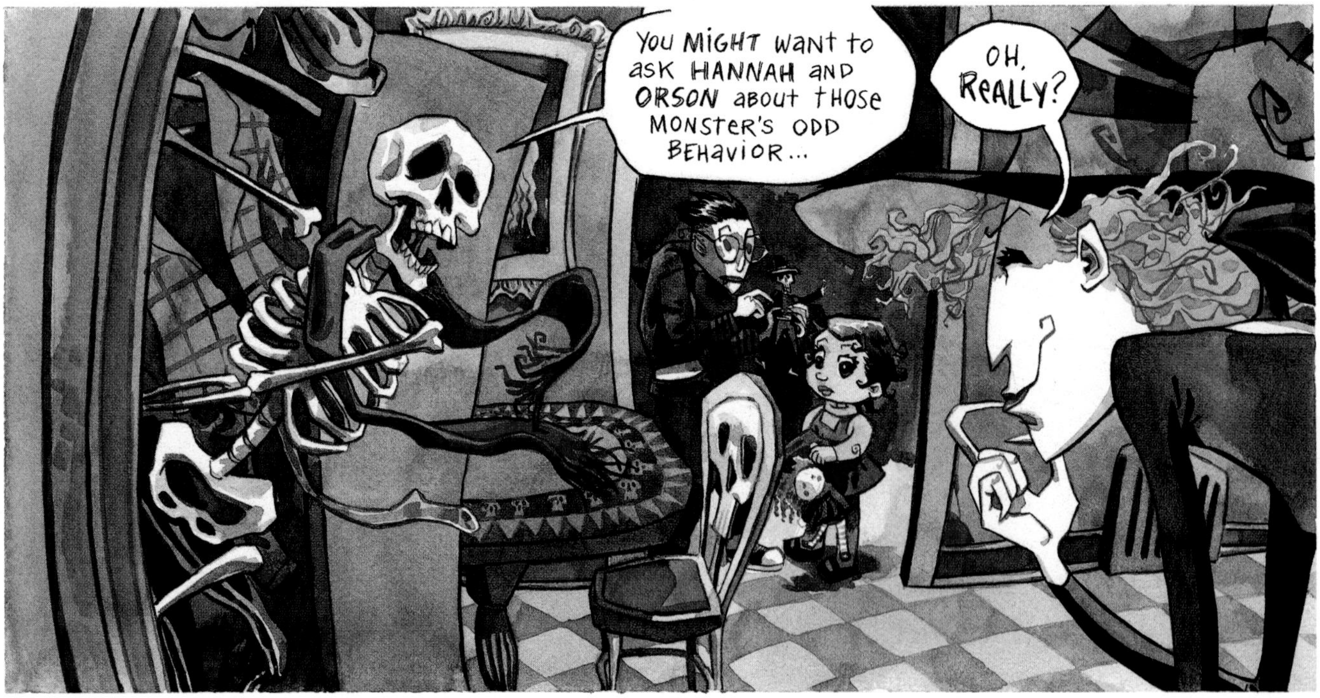
YOU MIGHT WANT TO ASK HANNAH AND ORSON ABOUT THOSE MONSTER'S ODD BEHAVIOR...
OH, REALLY?

Hannah and Orson 'fessed up as Bug-A-Boo came home.

And so, the Scary Godmother...ventured...outside to set things straight.

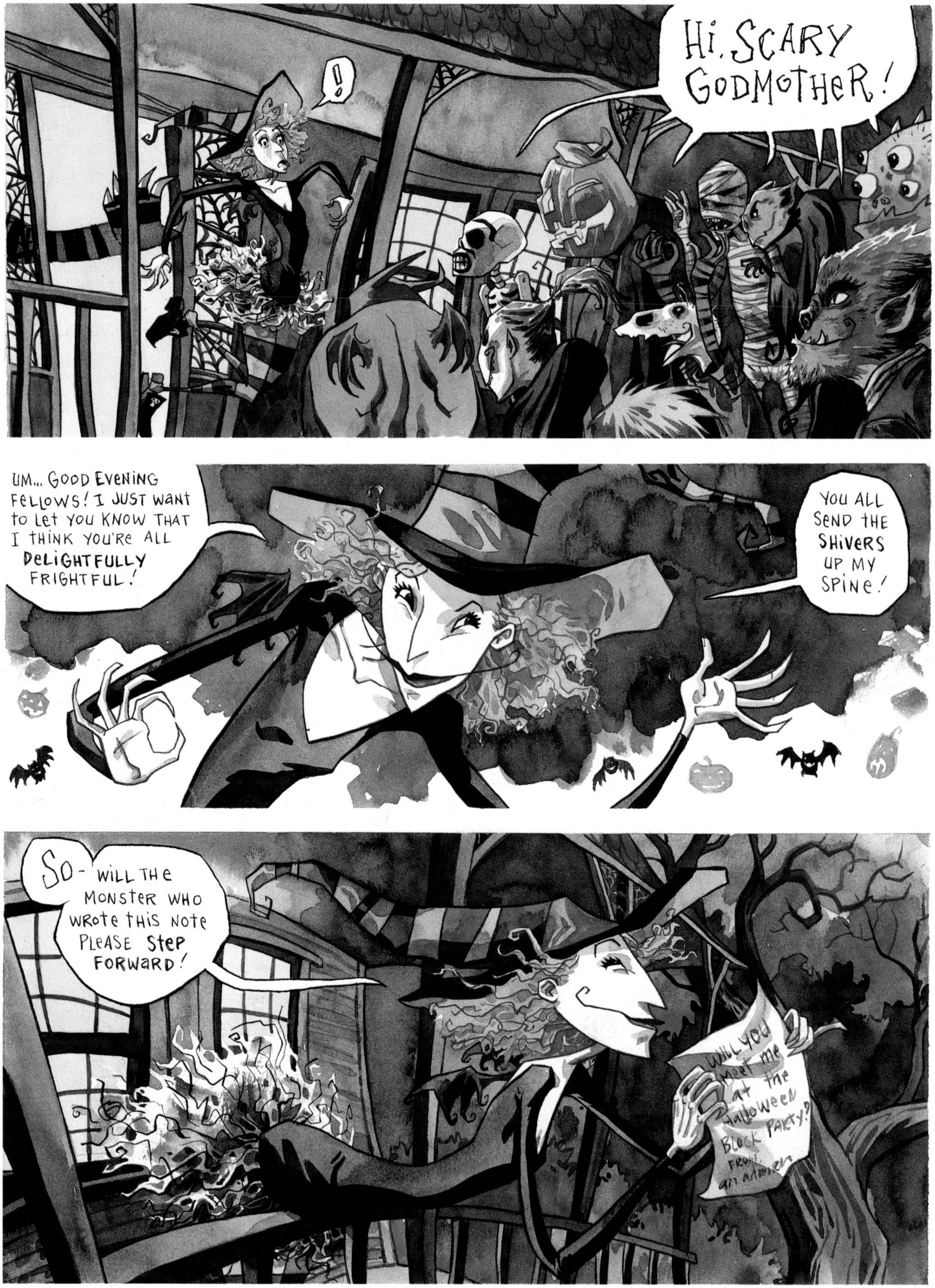
!
Hi, SCARY GODMOTHER!
UM... GOOD EVENING FELLOWS! I JUST WANT TO LET YOU KNOW THAT I THINK YOU'RE ALL DELIGHTFULLY FRIGHTFUL!
YOU ALL SEND THE SHIVERS UP MY SPINE!
SO- WILL THE MONSTER WHO WROTE THIS NOTE PLEASE STEP FORWARD!
Will you meet me at the Halloween Block Party?
From,

From nightmare to ghoul, the paper was passed around.

Amongst all of these monsters, the author was not found!

"Not me! Not me!" each monster explained as they took to the air or shambled back to coffins and caves.

The Scary Godmother exclaimed once they were out of sight...

On Halloween Day, Hannah's street was blocked off, so cars could not drive down it. Each family brought their treats and decorations to the sidewalk and by nightfall, the Haunted carnival was complete.

Hannah slipped on her costume and ran lickety-split, out to join the fun.

And what did our Scary Godmother do? Well, she got all gussied up!

From her head...

... to her toes.

She dressed in her most witchified, Hallow's Eve clothes! (with all of the necessary accessor-aries...)

When the Monsters arrived...

...they chased children with glee!

While the Scary Godmother stood waiting under a tree.

She waited...

...and waited...

...and waited.

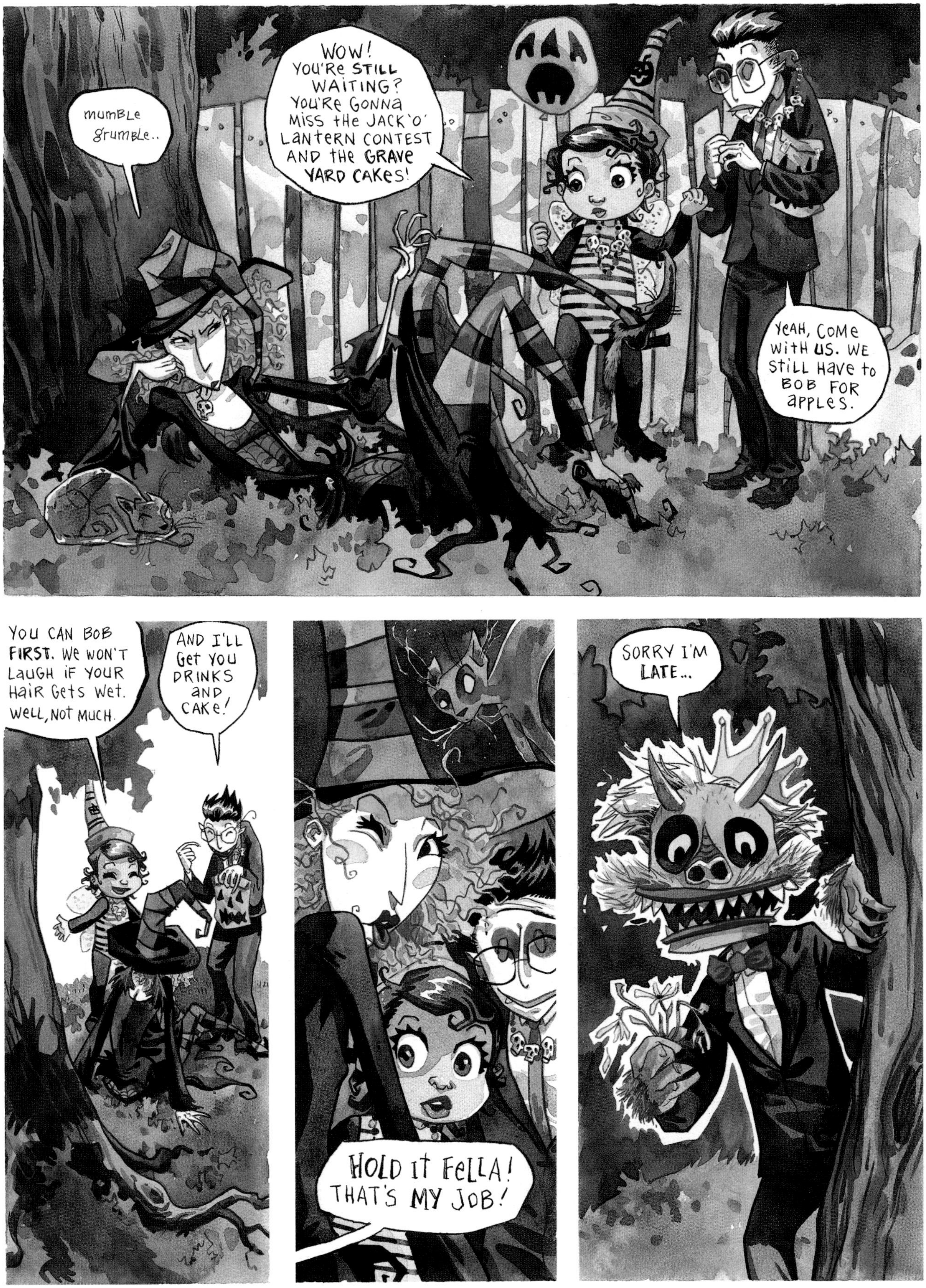
mumble grumble..
WOW! YOU'RE STILL WAITING? YOU'RE GONNA MISS THE JACK-'O' LANTERN CONTEST AND THE GRAVE YARD CAKES!
YEAH, COME WITH US. WE STILL HAVE TO BOB FOR APPLES.
YOU CAN BOB FIRST. WE WON'T LAUGH IF YOUR HAIR GETS WET. WELL, NOT MUCH.
AND I'LL GET YOU DRINKS AND CAKE!
HOLD IT FELLA! THAT'S MY JOB!
SORRY I'M LATE...

It was Jimmy who stepped up to escort the Scary Godmother to the festivities! He had said that he'd bring something none of the other kids would guess...and boy, was he right! He brought a Date!

Anyone could say they've brought a favorite cake or treat to a party...but how many could claim to have brought the Queen of Halloween?

So the King of the Monsters and his Halloween Queen enjoyed their All Hallow's evening.

Refreshments were in order after all of that fun, so the creepy couple crept over to the table of treats.

But when they got there...

THE END

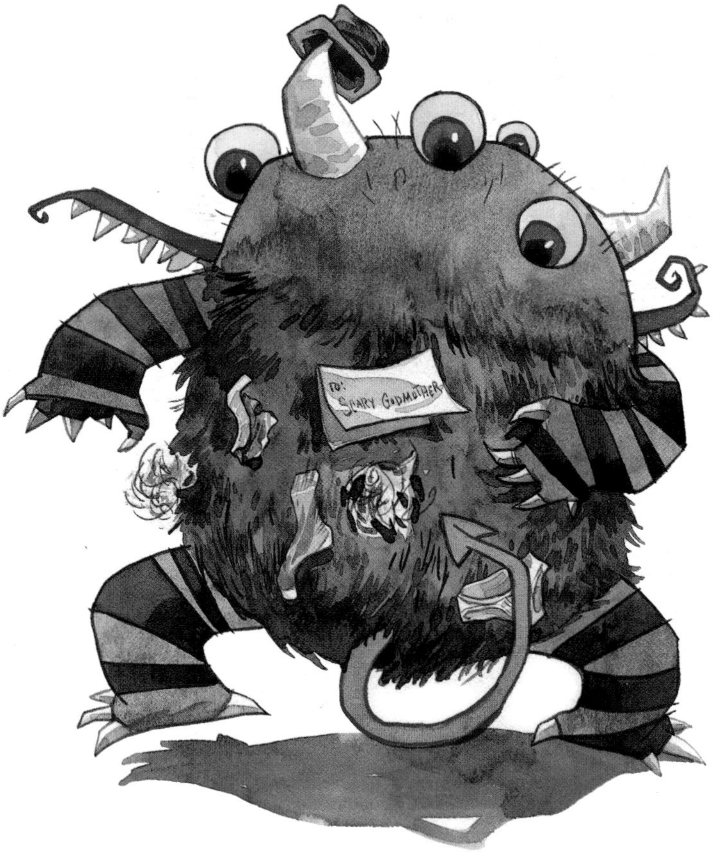
To: SCARY GODMOTHER